Letterland™

Contents

T0352615

Level 1   Student Book 1

Story ➡️ Let's meet Sammy Snake. Listen and repeat his name, sound and some words that start with his sound.

Track 2

Hi. My name is Sammy Snake.

Letter sound

Sammy Snake's sound is at the start of his name – **S**ammy **S**nake.

**Sound**

Look for the things in the picture that start with his sound. Then complete the exercises in *Workbook 1*.

Workbook

Sammy Snake says, S. He starts words like...

sun

sea

sand

**Action**

Do the action and say the rhythmic chant together!

Move and chant!

Sss, sss, sss.
Sammy Snake! (x2)

Multi-sensory

Make snake movements with your hand and arm.

Song Listen to the Alphabet Song. If you can, join in as you listen for the second time.

Sing and point!

Sammy Snake, sss,

Sammy Snake, sss,

Sammy Snake, Sammy Snake,

Sammy Snake, sss.

Sss. (x2)

sss...

Sammy Snake sometimes says, **ZZZ**.

In words like...

is   his   has

Sammy Snake is needed in so many words that sometimes he gets tired and has a quick snooze. Often this is at the END of words. Instead of his usual hissing sound you'll hear him snoozing 'zzz'.

Now you have completed all the sound activities in your *Student Book*, complete the sound activities in your *Workbook* too.

Uppercase Sammy Snake takes a deep breath and gets bigger.

 # Let's finger-trace!

Track 5

Hello. What's your name?

My name is Sarah.

What's your name?

I'm Sam.

Now it's your turn!

Get Creative

Further activity suggestions can be found in your *Fix-it Phonics Teacher's Guide*.

Role-play Practise in pairs. Repeat the exercise frequently to improve fluency.

Track 6

Hello. My name is Annie Apple.

Letter sound Annie Apple's sound is at the start of her name – **A**nnie **A**pple.

Look for the things in the picture that start with her sound.
Then complete the exercises in *Workbook 1*.

 Annie Apple says, **a.**
She starts words like...

ant

apple

arrow

 **Action**

Do the action and say the rhythmic chant together!

Move and chant!
A, a,
a, a, a,
Annie Apple! (x2)

 Multi-sensory Bite into an imaginary apple.

Song ➤ Listen to the Alphabet Song. If you can, join in as you listen for the second time.

Sing and point!

Annie Apple, she says, a, she says, a, she says, a.

Annie Apple, she says, a.

A, a, a. (x2)

A, a, a. A, a, a.

a...

Workbook

Now you have completed all the sound activities in your *Student Book,* complete the sound activities in your *Workbook* too.

Workbook

9

Uppercase Annie Apple sits on an apple stand with her friends.

 # Let's finger-trace!

A a

Uppercase letters You will see uppercase letters at the start of sentences, names or places. Practise writing the letters in *Workbook 1*.

Workbook

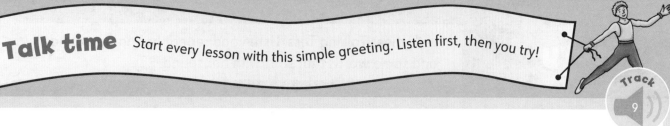

Track 9

How are you?

I'm fine, thank you.

How are you?

I'm fine, thanks.

Now it's your turn!

Get Creative

Further activity suggestions can be found in your *Fix-it Phonics Teacher's Guide.*

Role-play Practise this simple greeting in pairs.
Repeat the exercise frequently to improve fluency.

Let's meet Talking Tess. Listen and repeat her name, sound and some words that start with her sound.

Hello. My name is Talking Tess.

Letter sound Talking Tess's sound is at the start of her name – **T**alking **T**ess.

Sound Look for the things in the picture that start with her sound. Then complete the exercises in *Workbook 1*.

 Workbook

 Track 10

Talking Tess says, t.

She starts words like...

table

toys

10
ten

Action Do the action and say the rhythmic chant together!

 Track 11

Move and chant!

T, t, t.

Talking Tess! (x2)

Multi-sensory Lift your arms horizontally to make a T-shape.

Song  Listen to the Alphabet Song. If you can, join in as you listen for the second time.

 Track 12

Sing and point!  t

t...

Talking Tess says, t, t.

Talking Tess says, t.

Talking Tess says, t, t.

Talking Tess says, t.

Talking Tess, t, t.

Talking Tess, t, t.

Talking Tess says, t, t.

Talking Tess

says, t. (x2)

Workbook

Now you have completed all the sound activities in your Student Book, complete the sound activities in your *Workbook* too.

 Workbook

Uppercase → Talking Tess gets so tall that we can't see her head in the clouds.

 **Let's finger-trace!**

T t

Uppercase letters You will see uppercase letters at the start of sentences, names or places. Practise writing the letters in *Workbook 1*.

 Workbook

15

Track 13

circle

triangle

square

What is it?

It's a triangle.

Now it's your turn!

Get Creative

Further activity suggestions can be found in your *Fix-it Phonics Teacher's Guide.*

Role-play Practise in pairs to improve fluency and consolidate language. Take turns asking and answering the questions.

Story ➡️ Let's meet Peter Puppy. Listen and repeat his name, sound and some words that start with his sound.

Track 14

Hi. My name is Peter Puppy.

Letter sound 🏳️ Peter Puppy's sound is at the start of his name – **P**eter **P**uppy.

Sound

Look for the things in the picture that start with his sound. Then complete the exercises in *Workbook 1*.

Workbook

Peter Puppy says, **p**.
He starts words like...

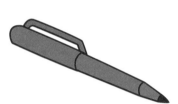 pen

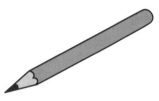 paint

pencil

Action

Stroke down imaginary ears.

Move and chant!

P, p, p.
P, p, p.
Peter Puppy!   (x2)

Multi-sensory Linking the sound to an action creates a great multisensory recall route for remembering the letter's sound.

Song ➡ Listen to the Alphabet Song. If you can, join in as you listen for the second time.

Track 16

Sing and point!

Peter Puppy, he says, p,
he says, p, he says, p.

Peter Puppy, he says, p,
he says, p.   (x2)
He says, p.
He says, p.

Uppercase

Peter Puppy jumps up
on to the line.

Let's finger-trace!

P p

Uppercase letters

You will see uppercase letters at the start of sentences, names or places. Practise writing the letters in *Workbook 1*.

Workbook

Point and play!

pink

blue

green

yellow

orange

red

It's your turn!

I like

I like pink.

Get Creative

Further activity suggestions can be found in your *Fix-it Phonics Teacher's Guide.*

Pair work Work in pairs. Tell your partner the colour you like most. Change partners and repeat.

Blending

> Oral blending. Make the individual sounds.
> Then start to blend the sounds to make the word.

s a t

sat →

Sound Slide

Try using the Sound Slide.
For further details see
Fix-it Phonics Teacher's Guide.

Word Building

> Use the *Big Picture Code Cards* to build the words below or enjoy the Word Building activity on *Phonics Online*.

 Code Card

at   sat

pat   tap

Word Building It's not important for children to understand the meaning of all of these words yet. Just focus on blending the sounds.

Read the stories in *Phonics Readers 1*, featuring the phonic elements in this *Student Book*.

Comprehension

Sss!

Focus on: s, a, t, p

Point to the character that did not like the tapping noise in the story.

Pat, pat!

Focus on: s, a, t, p

Point to the character that tried to pat the ants off in the story.

Workbook

Workbook

Now complete the writing and listening exercises in your *Workbook*.

Pair work

When you have read the stories, the teacher will read the questions. Work in pairs or small groups to read and point to the correct answers.

Story ➔ Let's meet Impy Ink. Listen and repeat his name, sound and some words that start with his sound.

Track 19

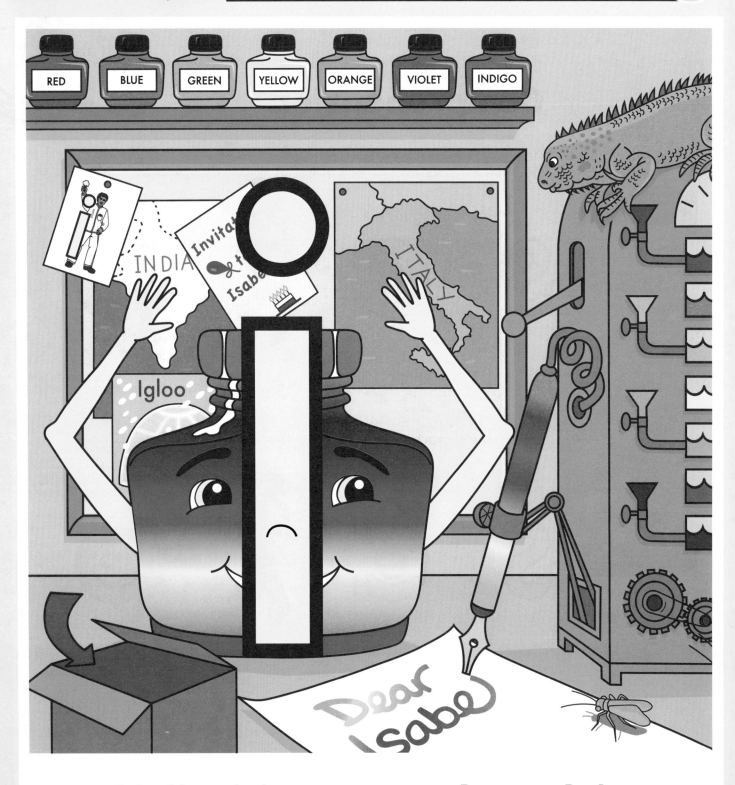

Hello. My name is Impy Ink.

Letter sound Impy Ink's sound is at the start of his name – **Impy Ink.**

Sound

Look for the things in the picture that start with his sound. Then complete the exercises in *Workbook 1*.

Workbook  Track 19

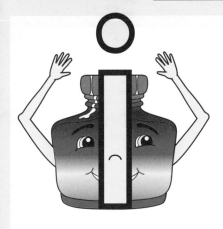

Impy Ink says, i.
He starts words like...

in

INDIGO

ink

insect

Move and chant!

I, i, i, i, i, i.
Impy Ink! (x2)

Song ➤ Listen to the Alphabet Song. If you can, join in as you listen for the second time.

Sing and point!

Impy Ink says, i, i,

i, i, i, i.

Impy Ink says, i, i.

He says, i. (x3)

Now you have completed all the sound activities in your *Student Book*, complete the sound activities in your *Workbook* too.

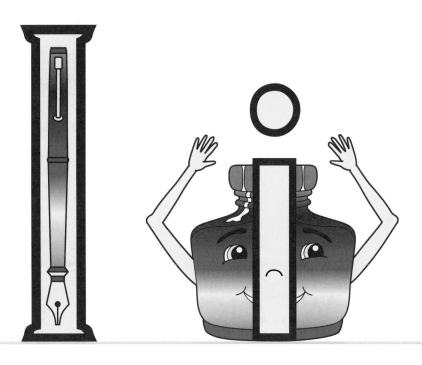

Uppercase Impy Ink takes a deep breath and gets tall and thin like an ink pen.

 ## Let's finger-trace!

Uppercase letters You will see uppercase letters at the start of sentences, names or places. Practise writing the letters in *Workbook 1*.

Workbook

27

Track 22

What is it?

It's an apple.

What is it?

It's an apple.

Now it's your turn!

Get Creative
Further activity suggestions can be found in the *Fix-it Phonics Teacher's Guide*.

Role-play Practise in pairs with objects you have learned so far by pointing at things in the room.

Story Let's meet Noisy Nick. Listen and repeat his name, sound and some words that start with his sound.

Track 23

Happy Birthday!

Hello. My name is Noisy Nick.

Letter sound Noisy Nick's sound is at the start of his name – **N**oisy **N**ick.

29

Sound ⟩ Look for the things in the picture that start with his sound. Then complete the exercises in *Workbook 1*.

Workbook | Track 23

Noisy Nick says, **n.**
He starts words like...

nine

nose

noodles

Action ⟩ Do the action and say the rhythmic chant together!

Track 24

Move and chant!

Nnn, nnn, Noisy Nick!
Nnn, nnn, Noisy Nick!

Multi-sensory | Bang one fist on the other, as if hammering a nail.

Song Listen to the Alphabet Song. If you can, join in as you listen for the second time.

Track 25

Sing and point!

n

Noisy Nick, nnn,
Noisy Nick, nnn,
Noisy Nick, Noisy Nick,
Noisy Nick, nnn.   (x2)

Workbook Now you have completed all the sound activities in your *Student Book*, complete the sound activities in your *Workbook* too.

Workbook

31

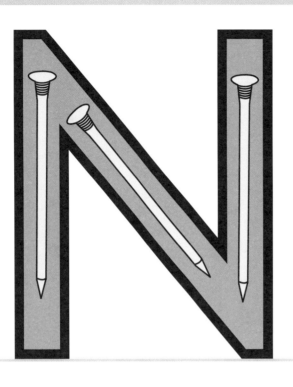

Uppercase Noisy Nick uses three nails to make his uppercase letter shape.

 # Let's finger-trace!

N n

Uppercase letters You will see uppercase letters at the start of sentences, names or places. Practise writing the letters in *Workbook 1.*

1 2 3 4 5 6 7 8 9

How old are you?

I'm five.

How old are you?

I'm six.

I'm nine!

Get Creative

Further activity suggestions can be found in the *Fix-it Phonics Teacher's Guide*.

Role-play Practise this exercise in pairs. Change partners and repeat.
Repeat the exercise frequently to improve fluency.

Story ➡️ Let's meet Munching Mike. Listen and repeat his name, sound and some words that start with his sound.

Track 27

Hi. My name is Munching Mike.

Letter sound — Munching Mike's sound is at the start of his name – **M**unching **M**ike.

Sound ▶ Look for the things in the picture that start with his sound. Then complete the exercises in *Workbook 1*.

Workbook  Track 27

Munching Mike says **m**.

He starts words like...

map **milk** **man**

Action ▶ Do the action and say the rhythmic chant together! Track 28

Move and chant!

Mmm, mmm.
Munching Mike! (x2)

 Multi-sensory Rub your tummy in a circular movement.

Song Listen to the Alphabet Song. If you can, join in as you listen for the second time.

Track 29

Sing and point!

Munching Mike says, mmm.

Munching Mike says, mmm.

Munching Mike says, mmm.

He says, mmm.　　(x2)

mmm…

Uppercase → Munching Mike's mum is much bigger than Mike, so she helps him start important words and sentences.

 **Let's finger-trace!**

M m

Uppercase letters You will see uppercase letters at the start of sentences, names or places. Practise writing the letters in *Workbook 1*.

 Workbook

37

Revise your numbers!

How many?

Oral language Count the objects on each line. Then take turns asking, "How many (maps)?"

Story Let's meet Dippy Duck. Listen and repeat her name, sound and some words that start with her sound.

Hello. My name is Dippy Duck.

Letter sound Dippy Duck's sound is at the start of her name – **D**ippy **D**uck.

Sound

Look for the things in the picture that start with her sound. Then complete the exercises in *Workbook 1*.

Dippy Duck says, d.
She starts words like...

dog

drum

dad

Action

Do the action and say the rhythmic chant together!

Move and chant!

D, d,
d, d, d.
Dippy Duck!   (x2)

Multi-sensory   Flap your elbows like a waddling duck.

Song ➤ Listen to the Alphabet Song. If you can, join in as you listen for the second time.

Sing and point!

Dippy Duck says, d, d,

Dippy Duck says, d, d,

Dippy Duck says, d, d,

Dippy Duck says, d.   (x3)

Workbook

Now you have completed all the sound activities in your *Student Book*, complete the sound activities in your *Workbook* too.

Workbook

41

Uppercase ➡ Dippy Duck goes behind her duck door.

 # Let's finger-trace!

D d

Uppercase letters You will see uppercase letters at the start of sentences, names or places. Practise writing the letters in *Workbook 1*.

Workbook

Talk time Days of the week. Listen first, then you try!

Listen and point!

MY DIARY

Thursday

Monday

Friday

Tuesday

Saturday

Wednesday

Sunday

Get Creative

Further activity suggestions can be found in the *Fix-it Phonics Teacher's Guide*.

Listen Listen to the days of the week. Join in when you listen again.
When is Dippy Duck coming to visit?

Oral blending. Make the individual sounds.
Then start to blend the sounds to make the word.

man
→

Sound Slide

Try using the Sound Slide.
For further details see
Fix-it Phonics Teacher's Guide.

Word Building

Use the *Big Picture Code Cards* to build the words below or
enjoy the Word Building activity on Phon*ics Online.*

Code
Card

an   man

pan   tan

Word
Building

It's not important for children to understand the meaning of all of
these words yet. Focus on blending and segmenting the sounds.

Read the stories in *Phonics Readers 2*, featuring the phonic elements in this *Student Book*.

Comprehension

Point to the correct answer.

1. Who tells Pat to sit?

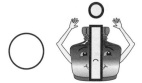 

2. Where is Nip?

○ In a pan.   ☐ In a tap.

3. What did Munching Mike grab in this story?

○ A man.   ☐ A map.

4. Choose the correct sentence to describe the sand in the story.

○ The sand is sad.

☐ The sand is damp.

Workbook

Now complete the writing and listening exercises in your *Workbook*.

Pair work

When you have read the stories, the teacher will read the questions.
Work in pairs or small groups to read and point to the correct answers.

Track 36

Hi. My name is Golden Girl.

Letter sound — Golden Girl's sound is at the start of her name – **G**olden **G**irl.

Sound ➤ Look for the things in the picture that start with her sound. Then complete the exercises in *Workbook 1*.

Golden Girl says, **g**.

She starts words like...

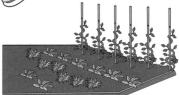  

garden **gate** **grass**

Action ➤ Do the action and say the rhythmic chant together!

Move and chant!

G, g, g, g.
Golden Girl! (x2)

 Multi-sensory — Mime holding a glass of grape juice in a 'glug, glug' position.

Song Listen to the Alphabet Song. If you can, join in as you listen for the second time.

Track 38

Sing and point!

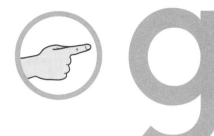

g

Golden Girl, she says g,

she says g, she says g.

Golden Girl, she says g,

Golden Girl says g.   (x2)

g...

Workbook

Now you have completed all the sound activities in your *Student Book*, complete the sound activities in your *Workbook* too.

Workbook

Uppercase

Golden Girl gets
into her go-cart to start important words.

Let's finger-trace!

G g

Uppercase letters You will see uppercase letters at the start of sentences, names or places. Practise writing the letters in *Workbook 1*.

Workbook

49

Track 39

Girls and boys!

girls

boys

I'm a girl.

I'm a girl.

I'm a boy.

Now it's your turn!

Get Creative

Further activity suggestions can be found in the *Fix-it Phonics Teacher's Guide*.

Oral language Practise in pairs. Change partners and repeat.

Story ➡

Let's meet Oscar Orange. Listen and repeat his name, sound and some words that start with his sound.

Track 40

Hi. My name is Oscar Orange.

Letter sound — Oscar Orange's sound is at the start of his name – **O**scar **O**range.

Look for the things in the picture that start with his sound. Then complete the exercises in *Workbook 1*.

 Oscar Orange says, O.

He starts words like...

on　　　　　**off**　　　　　**orange**

 **Action**

Do the action and say the rhythmic chant together!

Move and chant!

O, o,

O, o, o,

Oscar Orange! (x2)

 Multi-sensory

Form circles with your mouth and hand and look surprised.

Song Listen to the Alphabet Song. If you can, join in as you listen for the second time.

Track 42

Sing and point!

O, Oscar Orange,
o, Oscar Orange.

I'm o, Oscar Orange

Oscar Orange, o.   (x2)

o...

Workbook
Now you have completed all the sound activities in your *Student Book*, complete the sound activities in your *Workbook* too.

Workbook

53

Uppercase → Oscar Orange takes a deep breath and gets bigger.

 # Let's finger-trace!

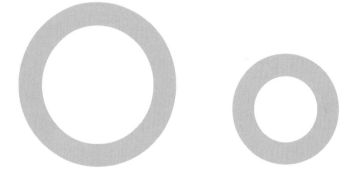

Uppercase letters You will see uppercase letters at the start of sentences, names or places. Practise writing the letters in *Workbook 1*.

Workbook

Listen and finger-trace!

up

down

around

down

up

around

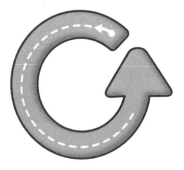

around

up

down

Oral language Repeat the words as you trace over the shapes with your finger. Describe how to form letter shapes with these new Keywords.

55

Story

Let's meet Clever Cat. Listen and repeat her name, sound and some words that start with her sound.

Track
44

Hello. My name is Clever Cat.

Letter sound

Clever Cat's sound is at the start of her name – **C**lever **C**at.

 Clever Cat says, C.
She starts words like...

car cup cake

Action Do the action and say the rhythmic chant together!

Move and chant!

C, c, Clever Cat!
C, c, Clever Cat!

Multi-sensory Stroke imaginary whiskers across your cheeks.

Song

Listen to the Alphabet Song. If you can, join in as you listen for the second time.

Track 46

Sing and point!  C

Clever Cat, she says c,
she says c, she says c.
Clever Cat, she says c,
Clever Cat says c.　(x2)

c...

Workbook

Now you have completed all the sound activities in your *Student Book*, complete the sound activities in your *Workbook* too.

Workbook

Uppercase

Clever Cat takes a deep breath and gets bigger.

Let's finger-trace!

Uppercase letters   You will see uppercase letters at the start of sentences, names or places. Practise writing the letters in *Workbook 1*.

Workbook

59

What can you do?

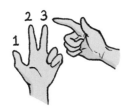

count   smile   wave   point

I can count.

I can smile.

Now it's your turn!

Get Creative

Further activity suggestions can be found in the *Fix-it Phonics Teacher's Guide*.

Pair work Take turns telling your partner what you can do.
Change partners and repeat.

Story

Let's meet Kicking King. Listen and repeat his name, sound and some words that start with his sound.

Track 48

Hello. My name is Kicking King.

Letter sound   Kicking King's sound is at the start of his name – **K**icking **K**ing.

61

Look for the things in the picture that start with his sound. Then complete the exercises in *Workbook 1*.

Kicking King says, k.
He starts words like...

  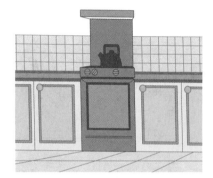

key   **kettle**   **kitchen**

Action ▶

Do the action and say the rhythmic chant together!

Move and chant!

K, k, k.
Kicking King!   (x2)

Multi-sensory   Lift up one arm and one leg to make a K-shape.

Song → Listen to the Alphabet Song. If you can, join in as you listen for the second time.

Sing and point!

Kicking King, Kicking King.

He says, k. He says, k.

Kicking King says, k, k.

Kicking King says, k, k.

He says, k.

He says, k.

Now you have completed all the sound activities in your *Student Book*, complete the sound activities in your *Workbook* too.

63

Uppercase Kicking King takes a deep breath and gets bigger.

 # Let's finger-trace!

K k

Uppercase letters You will see uppercase letters at the start of sentences, names or places. Practise writing the letters in *Workbook 1*.

Track 51

Let's play!

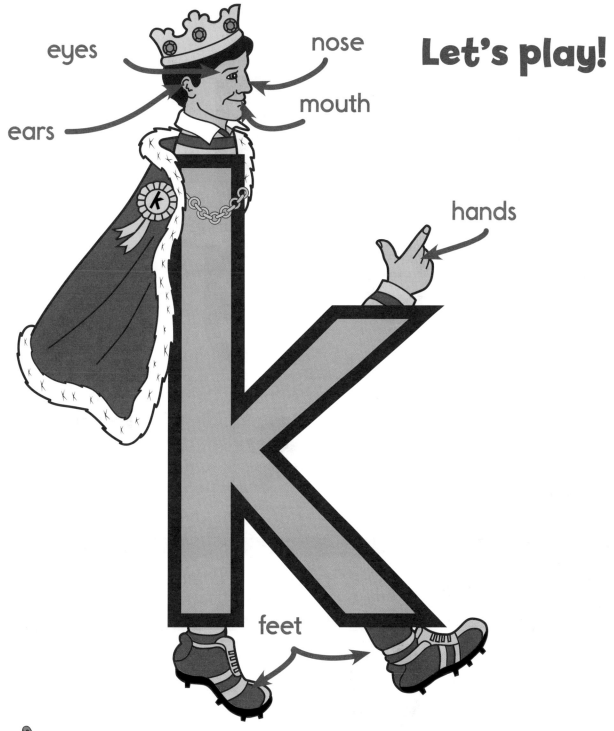

eyes

nose

mouth

ears

hands

feet

Get Creative!

Further activity suggestions can be found in the *Fix-it Phonics Teacher's Guide.*

Oral language Play Kicking King's game. Listen to Kicking King and point to your body when he tells you to.

Oral blending. Make the individual sounds.
Then start to blend the sounds to make the word.

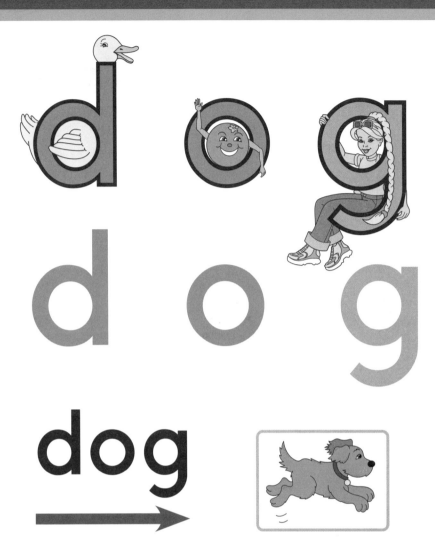

dog

Sound Slide

Try using the Sound Slide.
For further details see
Fix-it Phonics Teacher's Guide.

Word Building

Use the *Big Picture Code Cards* to build the words below or enjoy the Word Building activity on Phon*ics Online*.

Code
Card

on	dog
top	got

Red words = Keywords previously covered

Word Building

It's not important for children to understand the meaning of all of these words yet. Focus on blending and segmenting the sounds.

Phonics Readers

Read the stories in *Phonics Readers 3*, featuring the phonic elements in this *Student Book*.

Is it Dan?
and other stories

Four decodable stories

Comprehension

Point to the correct answer.

1. What does Dan do?

○ dig   ☐ dog

2. Is Tim a dog?

○ yes   ☐ no

3. Did Dad get Nat's hat?

○ yes   ☐ no

4. What did the king stop for?

○ a sit   ☐ a kiss

Workbook

Now complete the writing and listening exercises in your *Workbook*.

Pair work

When you have read the stories, the teacher will read the questions. Work in pairs or small groups to read and point to the correct answers.

Story ➤ Clever Cat and Kicking King make the same sound.
Clever Cat sits behind the King so she isn't kicked.

Track
53

Clever Cat and Kicking King

When they come together,
they both make their sound
at the same time.

Letter sound — Kicking King and Clever Cat both make the same sound.
They come together at the end of words.

Sound ➤ Listen to Clever Cat and Kicking King's words.
Complete the exercises in *Workbook 1*.

Workbook  Track 53

Clever Cat and Kicking King say **ck**, in words like...

kick   **sack**   **sock**

Action ➤ Do the action and say the rhythmic chant together!

 Track 54

Move and chant!

Ck, ck, ck, ck.
Ck, ck, ck, ck!   (x2)

 Multi-sensory Lift your leg as if to kick. Be very careful not to kick anyone!
Give yourself plenty of space.

 **Let's finger-trace!**

c k

ink dog map

kick sack sand

sock cat

insect milk

Letter shape Find and read all the **ck** words. Can you read the words? Complete the exercises in *Workbook 1*.

Workbook

Track 55

black

pink

blue

green

white

yellow

orange

red

What is it?

It's a sock.

What colour is it?

It's black.

Get Creative

Further activity suggestions can be found in the *Fix-it Phonics Teacher's Guide*.

Pair work Practise in pairs. Use the objects in the box above, use real objects or flashcards. Take turns asking the questions.

Story

Let's meet Eddy Elephant. Listen and repeat his name, sound and some words that start with his sound.

Track 56

Hi. My name is Eddy Elephant.

Letter sound Eddy Elephant's sound is at the start of his name – **E**ddy **E**lephant.

Sound

Look for the things in the picture that start with his sound. Then complete the exercises in *Workbook 1*.

Eddy Elephant says, e.
He starts words like...

egg   **envelope**   **elbow**

Action

Do the action and say the rhythmic chant together!

Move and chant!

E, e, e. E, e, e.
Eddy Elephant! (x2)

Multi-sensory   Spread your hands out as shown and flap them like elephant ears.

Song Listen to the Alphabet Song. If you can, join in as you listen for the second time.

Sing and point!

E, Eddy Elephant,
e, Eddy Elephant.

I'm e, Eddy Elephant,
Eddy Elephant, e. (x2)

Workbook Now you have completed all the sound activities in your *Student Book*, complete the sound activities in your *Workbook* too.

Shape

Make the shapes in the air. Then finger-trace them on this page.

Uppercase → Eddy Elephant sits on end.

 Let's finger-trace!

E e

Uppercase letters You will see uppercase letters at the start of sentences, names or places. Practise writing the letters in *Workbook 1*.

 Workbook

75

stand up

walk

run

sit down

swim

throw

Listen and do the action.

Track 59

It's your turn!

Let's exercise!

Get Creative

Further activity suggestions can be found in the *Fix-it Phonics Teacher's Guide.*

Oral language

Revise "I can…" in pairs with the new words.
"I can run, I can walk, etc."

Story

Let's meet Uppy Umbrella. Listen and repeat her name, sound and some words that start with her sound.

Track 60

Hi. My name is Uppy Umbrella.

Letter sound Uppy Umbrella's sound is at the start of her name – **U**ppy **U**mbrella.

77

Sound

Look for the things in the picture that start with her sound. Then complete the exercises in *Workbook 1*.

Uppy Umbrella says, U. She starts words like...

up

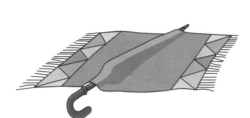

under

umbrella

Action

Do the action and say the rhythmic chant together!

Move and chant!

U, u, u. U, u, u. Uppy Umbrella! (x2)

Multi-sensory Hold up an imaginary umbrella with your hands as shown.

Song Listen to the Alphabet Song. If you can, join in as you listen for the second time.

Sing and point!

Uppy Umbrella, she says u,

she says u, she says u.

Uppy Umbrella, she says u.

Uppy Umbrella says u. (x 3)

Workbook Now you have completed all the sound activities in your *Student Book*, complete the sound activities in your *Workbook* too.

79

Uppercase ➤ Uppy Umbrella takes a deep breath and gets bigger.

 # Let's finger-trace!

U u

Uppercase letters — You will see uppercase letters at the start of sentences, names or places. Practise writing the letters in *Workbook 1*.

Workbook

under

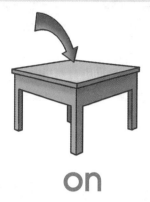

on

Where is the cat?

It's on the table.

Now it's your turn!

Get Creative

Further activity suggestions can be found in the *Fix-it Phonics Teacher's Guide*.

Pair work Practise in pairs to improve fluency and consolidate language. Use flashcards or real objects. Take turns asking where they are.

Story →

Let's meet Red Robot. Listen and repeat his name, sound and some words that start with his sound.

Track 64

Hello. My name is Red Robot.

Letter sound

Red Robot's sound is at the start of his name – **R**ed **R**obot.

Sound

Look for the things in the picture that start with his sound. Then complete the exercises in *Workbook 1*.

Workbook

 Track 64

Red Robot says, r.

He starts words like...

rain

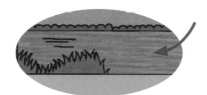

river

RICE

rice

Action

Do the action and say the rhythmic chant together!

 Track 65

Move and chant!

Rrr, rrr,
Red Robot!   (x2)

Song Listen to the Alphabet Song. If you can, join in as you listen for the second time.

Sing and point!

Red Robot, Red Robot,

says rrr, says rrr.

Red Robot, Red Robot,

says rrr, says rrr.   (x2)

rrr...   Rrrr.

Now you have completed all the sound activities in your *Student Book*, complete the sound activities in your *Workbook* too.

Uppercase Red Robot takes a deep breath, gets bigger and changes shape.

Let's finger-trace!

R r

Uppercase letters You will see uppercase letters at the start of sentences, names or places. Practise writing the letters in *Workbook 1*.

85

What can you do?

run   ride a bike   read

Can you read?

Yes, I can.

Now it's your turn!

Get Creative

Further activity suggestions can be found in the *Fix-it Phonics Teacher's Guide*.

Pair work Work in pairs asking the question, "Can you... ?"
Answer the question with, "Yes, I can." or "No, I can't."

Blending

Oral blending. Make the individual sounds.
Then start to blend the sounds to make the word.

r u n

run

Sound Slide

Try using the Sound Slide.
For further details see
Fix-it Phonics Teacher's Guide.

Word Building

Use the *Big Picture Code Cards* to build the words below
or enjoy the Word Building activity on *Phonics Online*.

Code
Card

net   run

men   cup

Red words = Keywords previously covered

Word Building It's not important for children to understand the meaning of these
words yet. Focus on blending and segmenting the sounds.

Read the stories in *Phonics Readers* 4, featuring the phonic elements in this *Student Book*.

Comprehension
Point to the correct answer.

1. What is the matter with Sam?

◯ He is hot.   ☐ He is sick.

2. In this story, how many times did you answer 'yes'?

1 2 3 4 5 6 7 8 9 10

3. What does Nick get?

◯ Nick gets nuts.

☐ Nick gets a cat.

4. What colour rug did Red Robot grab?

Workbook

Now complete the writing and listening exercises in your *Workbook*.

Well done! Now you can move on to *Student Book 2*!

Pair work

When you have read the stories, the teacher will read the questions. Work in pairs or small groups to read and point to the correct answers.